Financial Flourish: Mastering Money
Management for a Prosperous Future
Unlock the Secrets of Wealth Building, Smart
Saving, and Strategic Investing to Achieve
Financial Freedom

Jane J. Whitney

Table of content

Chapter 1

Introduction: Navigating the Path to Financial Prosperity

Chapter 2

Understanding Your Financial Landscape

Chapter 3

Budgeting Basics: Building the Foundation for Success

Chapter 4

Smart Saving Strategies: Growing Your Money Thoughtfully

Chapter 5

Debt Demystified: Breaking Free and Building Wealth

Chapter 6

The Art of Investing: Strategies for Long-Term Financial Growth

Chapter 7

Income Optimization: Maximizing Your Earning Potential

Chapter 8

Building a Resilient Financial Plan: Weathering Life's Storms

Chapter 9

Financial Literacy for a Sustainable Future

Chapter 10

Achieving Financial Freedom: Putting It All Together

Chapter 1

Introduction: Navigating the Path to Financial Prosperity

"Navigating the Path to Financial Prosperity," we're going to take a revolutionary step toward abundance and financial well-being. We'll lay the groundwork for your investigation of the ideas and methods that will lead you to financial success in these introductory chapters.

We will discuss the importance of financial prosperity and how it affects your life in general in the first few pages. Comprehending the significance of money in your goals, desires, and daily encounters is essential for effectively pursuing this route.

We'll talk about the mentality change needed to achieve financial success. Your financial journey is significantly influenced by the ideas and attitudes you have about money. Learn how to change your relationship with wealth and create new opportunities by adopting an abundance attitude.

To chart your course to prosperity, it is imperative that you make your financial objectives clear. We will assist you in establishing financial goals that are clear, quantifiable, and doable. Setting objectives is the compass that points you in the right direction, whether it's saving money, reducing debt, or investing.

Gaining knowledge of the finance language is empowering. Important financial concepts are explained in this area to provide you the information you need to make wise decisions. We'll set the stage for developing your financial literacy by covering everything from investing to budgeting.

A key component of financial success is budgeting. We'll look at doable tactics for setting up a budget that tracks your expenses, helps you reach your goals, and gives you financial autonomy.

Examine the fundamentals of protecting and accumulating wealth. This section gives you the tools to manage and expand your financial resources, from risk management to wise investments.

Having a sound foundation, an optimistic outlook, and the information necessary to make wise decisions are the first steps on your path to financial success. Prepare yourself to traverse the curves and turns of this life-changing journey toward success and financial well-being.

Chapter 2

Understanding Your Financial Landscape

Taking the first step toward financial literacy is essential to attaining long-term success and security. For novices, navigating the financial landscape can be intimidating, but with the appropriate information and strategy, it can be a gratifying and manageable experience. This beginner's book is to give people who want to take charge of their finances important insights and useful advice.

Recognize Your Income and Expenses: To begin, make a thorough budget that lists all of your monthly income and outlays.

Sort spending into necessities (such rent and utilities) and non-essentials (like entertainment and eating out).

You will be better able to budget funds and find places where you can save by having this clarity.

Create an Emergency Fund: A crucial first step is to create an emergency fund. Three to six months' worth of living expenditures should be your goal.

This fund serves as a safety net for finances, giving comfort in the event of unforeseen costs or job loss.

Investigate Various Savings and Investment Choices: Learn about certificates of deposit (CDs), savings accounts, and investment choices like stocks and bonds.

Investing in a diverse portfolio can help you control risk and even eventually boost rewards.

Credit Management: Acquire knowledge about credit ratings and their implications for your financial stability. To keep track of your credit history, get a free credit report once a year.

To take advantage of advantageous financial prospects, use credit wisely, pay your bills on time, and work to preserve a decent credit score.

Debt management: To prevent accruing excessive interest, give priority to paying off high-interest debt, such as credit card debt. Investigate your choices for consolidating debt and make a strategy for repayment to gradually lower your balances.

Financial Education and Resources: To improve your financial literacy, make use of books, classes, and internet resources.

Keep up with the latest developments in personal finance, investment techniques, and economic trends.

Retirement Planning: Get a head start on your retirement savings. Benefit from retirement programs offered by your work, such as pension or 401(k) plans.

Think about working with a financial advisor to design a customized retirement plan that fits your objectives.

Coverage for Insurance: Recognize the significance of insurance, including life, health, and property insurance.

Make sure your coverage is up to date and meets your needs now by reviewing it on a regular basis.

Set Financial Objectives: Make both short- and long-term financial objectives. This could include putting money aside for a trip, purchasing a house, or supporting a child's education.

For a more manageable approach, break down large goals into smaller, doable tasks.

Financial illiteracy refers to a lack of knowledge and understanding regarding financial matters. Individuals considered financially illiterate may struggle to comprehend fundamental financial concepts, make informed decisions about money, and effectively manage their personal finances. This lack of financial literacy can manifest in various ways, including challenges in budgeting, investing, debt management, and overall financial planning. Financial illiteracy can have significant consequences, leading individuals to make uninformed choices that may result in debt accumulation, missed investment opportunities, or inadequate preparation for long-term financial goals like retirement. Addressing financial illiteracy involves improving one's understanding of basic financial principles, developing sound money management skills, and making informed decisions to achieve financial well-being.

Case Study: The Credit Card Dilemma

Meet Sarah, a recent college graduate who landed her first job. Excited about her newfound financial independence, Sarah soon encountered the complexities of credit cards, becoming a poignant case study in financial illiteracy.

Background:

Fresh out of college, Sarah was offered a credit card with a seemingly attractive rewards program. Eager to build her credit and enticed by the promise of cash back, she signed up without fully understanding the implications.

Financial Illiteracy Manifests:

1. Misuse of Credit:

Sarah started using her credit card for everyday expenses without keeping track of her spending. The convenience of "buy now, pay later" became a slippery slope as she failed to recognize the accumulating balance.

2. Minimum Payments Trap:

Unaware of the consequences, Sarah fell into the minimum payments trap. She made only the minimum monthly payments, not realizing that the majority went towards interest, keeping her in a perpetual cycle of debt.

3.Interest Accumulation:

Financial illiteracy became evident when Sarah overlooked the high-interest rates associated with carrying a balance. Interest charges accrued, further escalating her debt.

Consequences:

1. Debt Spiral:

Sarah found herself in a mounting debt situation, struggling to keep up with credit card payments. The debt snowballed due to interest, hindering her financial progress.

2.Credit Score Impact:

Unbeknownst to Sarah, her accumulating debt had a detrimental impact on her credit score. This oversight would later affect her ability to secure favorable terms for loans or future credit.

Learning from the Case Study:

1.Importance of Understanding Terms:

Sarah's case underscores the critical need to understand the terms and conditions of financial products. Knowing the interest rates, fees, and consequences of credit card usage is essential.

2.Budgeting and Tracking Expenses:

Financial literacy involves budgeting and tracking expenses. Sarah's experience highlights the importance of creating a budget and diligently monitoring spending to avoid debt accumulation.

3.Educating on Credit Scores:

Understanding the significance of credit scores is vital. Sarah's lack of awareness about the impact of her financial choices on her credit score serves as a valuable lesson for others.

Conclusion:

Sarah's credit card dilemma exemplifies the real-world consequences of financial illiteracy. By learning from her mistakes, individuals can enhance their financial literacy, make informed decisions, and avoid falling into similar traps. This case study underscores the importance of education and awareness in navigating the complexities of personal finance.

In summary:

As a novice, navigating the financial world may seem difficult, but you can create a solid foundation for a safe financial future with commitment and wise decision-making.

Understanding your financial status, controlling your debt, and making strategic investments provide you the power to make prudent financial decisions that support your objectives. Your allies on this path to financial well-being will be proactive financial planning and ongoing learning.

Chapter 3

Budgeting Basics: Building the Foundation for Success

Effective budgeting is the smartest tool which when followed diligently enables us to manage our finances and to a large extent life stress free. It is a dynamic and indispensable financial tool that should be wholeheartedly embraced. It serves as a compass, adapting to one's respective life stage and cruising through the journey with minimal disruptions.

A well-crafted budget ideally provides an accurate representation of your financial path and sets you on the road to success. The fundamental principles of budgeting and strategies for individuals at various life stages differ and should be kept in mind while planning for the future.

Basic Guidelines for Budgeting:

Income Assessment: - Recognize your sources of income, such as investments, side jobs, and a regular wage.

Expense Identification: - Sort and arrange all of your expenses, making a distinction between fixed costs (rent, mortgage, etc.) and variable costs (entertainment, eating out, etc.).

Prioritize Essential Expenses: - Set aside a sizeable amount of your income for necessities such as housing, utilities, groceries, and medical care.

Allocation of Emergency Fund: - A percentage of your budget should be set aside for an emergency fund in order to meet unforeseen costs or financial setbacks.

Debt Management:- Make minimum payments on other bills to prevent interest from accruing, and give priority to paying off high-interest loans.

Investments and Savings:- Set aside money in your budget for investments and savings in order to accumulate wealth and meet long-term financial objectives.

Budget Flexibility:- Establish a budget that is adaptable to shifts in spending, income, or unforeseen circumstances.

Regular Monitoring: - Make sure your budget is in line with your changing lifestyle and financial objectives by reviewing and adjusting it on a regular basis.

Alignment of Financial Goals:- Make sure that your budget is in line with your long- and short-term financial objectives, such as retirement, homeownership, and education.

Continuous Learning:- To improve your financial literacy, stay up to date on investment alternatives, budgeting methods, and personal finance strategies.

By putting these core ideas into practice, you may create an effective budget that serves as a guide for reaching your financial goals and establishing financial stability.

Making a budget for oneself
How to Make and Stick to a Budget
Everyone can benefit from and practice creating and adhering to a budget. Making a budget is an effective way to create a financial plan, increase your financial competence, and feel more empowered with money.

How do you feel about creating a budget?

Your perspective may determine how well you do with budgeting. Budgets, according to some, are supposed to be limiting, to rob life of its joy, and to make you feel guilty about your purchases. Some people might think that creating or adhering to a budget takes too much effort or time.

Budgeting is actually a very empowering practice. It gives you the power to allocate your funds to the things in life that truly matter to you, like having fun. In light of this, it will be well worth your time to establish a reasonable budget that you can stick to.

A budget: what is it? What steps are included in budgeting?

A written plan outlining your monthly expenses and savings is called a budget. Among the things budgeting includes:

- Determining your objectives and priorities
- Drafting a budget that lists your projected monthly income and outlays
- Monitoring your real income and spending

- Modifying the plan

Why stick to a budget? Making a budget facilitates:

- Give you financial control and make sure your money is being used to fulfill your demands and accomplish your objectives.
- Reduce unnecessary spending and let you see where your money is going.
- Become more adept at paying all of your expenses and avoiding financial emergencies throughout the month.
- Set aside funds to settle debt
- Put money aside for the items you truly want.
- Decrease anxiety and boost self-assurance
- Be more emergency-ready

A budget may ***be created and used in five easy steps.***

Budgeting can be easy to understand and implement. To create and stick to a budget that works for you, use these guidelines. You could find this budget tool helpful when making your own.

First, calculate your monthly income.

Enumerate your sources of income and the monthly amount you anticipate receiving. You may receive money from Social Security, child support, gig labor earnings, paychecks, and other sources. To ensure success, estimate conservatively if the quantity of your income varies every period. Here's an illustration:

Income: $1,500 per check
Two paychecks totaling $1,500
The entire projected monthly revenue is $3,000.

Step 2: Determine how much you'll be spending each month.

How much money do you spend? Commence by making an estimate of your fixed expenses, or those that remain constant from month to month. Fixed expenses can include things like your garbage bill, rent or mortgage, and cell phone bill. Include a cost breakdown for each expense. Next, determine which of your monthly expenses are variable—that is, those with varying cash amounts. These costs include groceries, dining out, presents, clothing, and gas. Calculate your monthly spending for these. You can get more precise estimations of amounts by reviewing previous bank or credit card statements. Remember to account for annual expenses in your budget. Divide the cost by 12 to get a budget for these, then set away that sum every month. Once you're done, figure out your entire projected monthly spending. Take a look at the sample below.

Costs

Unchanged Costs

$1,400 in rent

Mobile phone$100

Trash$50 Auto Insurance$200

Changeable Costs

Food purchases: $400

Dining out: $100

$100 for clothing

$200 for gas and gifts$150

The total projected cost is $2,700.

Step 3: Evaluate your priorities and objectives while comparing your entire expected income and expenses.

Compare your projected total income and estimated total costs now. You anticipate having extra money if your anticipated monthly income is higher than your anticipated monthly costs. That's fantastic! The individual in the a fore mentioned scenario anticipates receiving $3,000 and spending $2,700 monthly. A $300 monthly excess is anticipated.

Talking about financial priorities and objectives now is a good idea. What financial goals do you have, either through investments or savings? When you can see yourself progressing and are able to allocate as much money as possible towards your goals, budgeting becomes fun. Establishing an emergency fund or putting money aside for a trip are examples of short-term savings objectives. Investing in retirement or saving for a down payment are examples of long-term objectives.

After deciding on your priorities and goals, think about the amount of time you will dedicate each month to achieving those objectives. The individual in the aforementioned scenario chooses to save aside $100 every month to increase their emergency fund. Additionally, the individual decides to fund an investing account with $200 each month. Try to set aside between 10 and 20 percent of your monthly income for savings and investments. The individual in the example intends to invest or save 10% of their monthly income ($300 / $3,000 = 10%).

You anticipate a deficit if your expected costs exceed your expected income. You will need to either raise your expected revenue or decrease your estimated expenses in order to handle this. Make choices that will help you balance your finances. Can you, for instance, figure out how to cut back on your monthly entertainment or grocery expenses? Or is it possible for you to work two jobs and make more money?

Step 4: Monitor your expenditures and determine whether you met your monthly budget at the end of the month.

Create a strategy to track your monthly expenses and determine whether you are adhering to your spending limit. Utilize the information to modify your spending plan or your budget at the end of the month. Did you have any unaccounted-for spending leaks? Does a new budget category need to be created? Do you need to change how much you set aside in your budget for specific costs? Do you need to make some financial adjustments? Have you reached your savings targets?

Over time, budgets should be modified. Do you really want to be spending and saving the money that I am? "Am I taking care of my needs and making progress toward my goals?" If you find that you are not spending as much money as you would like each month, think about modifying your budget so that you can use that extra money to accomplish additional or even earlier goals.

Step 5: Persist in it

With time, budgeting, conserving money, and identifying and sealing leaks in your expenditure become habits. Organize your life to succeed by:

- Establishing reasonable, attainable expectations and objectives
- Designing an easy-to-use and maintain monitoring system and budget
- Establishing recurrent transfers to investment or savings accounts to automate investing and saving

- Using techniques to curb impulsive
  buying and cultivate self-control

You will feel more capable of achieving your
objectives as you put in the time to practice,
develop good habits, make changes, and begin to
see results.

Free budget template

https://drive.google.com/file/d/1gi6eKKmHjd6D
7TsR4gFpu61X02owGBAe/view?usp=drivesdk

**Case Study: Emma's Journey to Financial
Empowerment through Budgeting**

Meet Emma, a young professional navigating the
complexities of her financial landscape. Her
story serves as a compelling case study,
illustrating the transformative power of
embracing budgeting basics for financial
empowerment.

Background:

Emma, fresh out of college and excited about her
first job, found herself facing the challenges of
managing her finances independently. With a
modest income and various financial aspirations,

she realized the need for a structured approach to her money.

Financial Struggles:

1. Unpredictable Spending:

   Emma's spending habits were erratic, with little consideration for where her money was going. She often found herself wondering where her paycheck went by the end of the month.

2. No Emergency Fund:

   Like many young adults, Emma didn't have an emergency fund. When faced with an unexpected car repair expense, she had to dip into her savings earmarked for other goals, disrupting her financial plans.

Emma Embraces Budgeting:

Recognizing the need for change, Emma decided to embrace budgeting as a tool for financial empowerment.

Steps Taken:

1. Income Assessment:

   Emma started by carefully assessing her income. This involved understanding her take-home pay and any additional sources of income.

2. Expense Categorization:

She categorized her expenses into fixed (rent, utilities) and variable (entertainment, dining out) to gain clarity on her spending patterns.

3.Creating a Budget:

Emma developed a realistic budget that allocated funds for essentials, savings, and discretionary spending. She set aside a portion for an emergency fund, aiming to build financial resilience.

4. Monitoring and Adjusting:

Emma actively tracked her expenses, using budgeting apps to stay organized. Regular reviews allowed her to identify areas where adjustments were needed.

Positive Outcomes:

1.Financial Awareness:

Through budgeting, Emma gained a profound awareness of her financial habits. She understood the value of each dollar and became intentional about her spending.

2.Emergency Fund:

Building an emergency fund provided Emma with peace of mind. When faced with unexpected expenses, she had the financial cushion to handle them without derailing her long-term goals.

3. Goal Achievement:

Emma's budget became a roadmap to achieving her financial goals. Whether saving for a vacation or contributing to a retirement fund, she saw tangible progress.

Conclusion:

Emma's journey exemplifies the transformative impact of embracing budgeting basics. By taking control of her finances, she not only overcame immediate challenges but set herself on a path to long-term financial success. Her case study underscores the empowerment that comes from understanding, planning, and actively managing one's budget.

Chapter 4

Smart Saving Strategies: Growing Your Money Thoughtfully

The biggest issue with saving is that, even though it's common knowledge that having money carefully set aside for the future is a good idea, it may be highly alluring to spend what you already have on the things you want, right now. The other issue is that it's always extremely easy to believe that there will be plenty of time to start saving—later—because the future always looks so far off.

It's possible that the future is closer than you believe! It is advisable to begin saving as soon as possible since you could lose your work, get sick, or get hurt. You won't regret saving as much as you can when you can. Avoid making frequent purchases on credit; it's an unnecessary spending habit. Use a money transfer provider to send money overseas at a significantly lower cost than paying exorbitant bank fees. Save now, instead of telling yourself you'll start next month.The Value of Saving Money

You may increase your financial security and independence by saving money. If you have a sizable savings account, you won't have to rely solely on your paycheck each month to live a comfortable life and achieve your goals and objectives. You can make important life decisions, like changing jobs, going on a vacation, getting married, or launching your own business, without worrying if you have enough savings to fall back on.

The ideal course of action is to develop the habit of saving as early as possible. It could seem a little challenging at first. However, you will be inspired to increase your savings rate as you begin to realize the fruits of your labor.

Shrewd financial advice

If you follow these money-saving advice on a daily basis, you'll eventually reach financial security. You can enlist a friend or family member to accompany you on this adventure and serve as your accountability partner. Here are simple methods to save costs:

Keep a record of your spending.

The majority of people lament that they are clueless about where their monthly funds are going. Being aware of your daily spending habits and where you spend your money is essential to maintaining your financial goals. The secret is to keep track of all of your transactions, including the amount of money you take in and spend. A money-tracking tool can help you automate the procedure.

When you track your expenses over a period of six to twelve months, you will see a definite pattern in your spending, and having access to this data will make financial planning much easier.

Observe the 50-30-20 rule.

The key to following this guideline is to be aware of your basic requirements and desires, be able to pay off debt, and begin saving. This rule states that you should allocate 50% of your monthly income toward your "needs," which typically include fixed costs like rent, utilities, groceries, clothing, transportation, medications, and necessary bills; 30% of your income can be allocated toward "wants" like eating out, taking trips, and shopping; and 20% should be allocated toward savings and investments. This guideline helps those who have trouble managing their budget to stay on top of their spending and save money for a rainy-day fund.Reducing impulsive purchases

You might not be aware of this, but impulse purchases frequently account for a sizable portion of your disposable cash. It might be getting takeout when you're too busy to cook or purchasing an unnecessary new clothing. You can better understand the effects of impulsive purchases on your financial situation by keeping track of your spending. With this information, you may reduce impulsive purchases and make better-informed financial decisions.

One essential component of sound financial management is saving money.

Here are some useful money-saving advice:

1. Make a Budget: Create a budget to help you understand your income, fixed costs (such as utilities and rent), and variable costs (like

groceries and entertainment). This assists you in determining where you may make savings.

2. Set Savings Goals:Establish definite, attainable goals for your savings. Setting specific goals, such as saving for a down purchase, a trip, or an emergency fund, helps you stay motivated.

3. Automate Savings:Configure your checking and savings accounts to make automatic transfers. Your salary will go directly into savings thanks to automation, which eliminates the need for ongoing human labor.

4.Track Your expenditures:Keep a close eye on your expenditures to see any areas where you might be going overboard. Making educated decisions on where to make cuts is facilitated by tracking.

5.Reduce Impulse Buys: Hold off on making impulsive purchases. Determine whether you need it or whether you just want it. You can avoid making impulsive purchases by delaying non-essential purchases.

6.Cook at Home: Frequent dining out might put a strain on your finances. Not only is home cooking more economical, but it's also healthier.

Create grocery lists, plan your meals, and follow them.

7. Shop Wisely: Before making any purchases, check for deals, use coupons, and compare costs. If you want to save money on particular things without sacrificing quality, think about purchasing generic brands.

8. Negotiate Bills: Talk about negotiating regular expenses like internet, cable, and insurance. Discounts or better offers could be made by providers, particularly if you've been a consistent customer.

9. Establish a Fund for Emergencies:
   Establish an emergency fund as a top priority to pay for unforeseen costs. When financial times are bad, having a safety net lessens the need to turn to credit or loans.

10. Examine Your Subscriptions:
    Examine your subscription services on a regular basis. If you don't use them often, downgrade or cancel them. This covers periodicals, streaming services, and other subscription services.

11. Reduction in Transportation Expenses:

Examine affordable modes of transportation. To reduce your fuel and maintenance expenses, think about carpooling, using the bus or train, or riding your bike.

12. Compare Service Companies:

Compare utility companies on a regular basis for services like internet, gas, and electricity. Sometimes switching providers can result in more favorable prices and offers.

13. Prevent Debt Buildup:Use credit cards sparingly for non-essential expenditures. As soon as you can, pay off high-interest debt to prevent having to make additional extra payments.

14. Make Use of Benefits Provided by Employers:

If your work provides perks like a 401(k) match, make sure you invest enough to get the most out of it. It's an additional means of financial support for retirement savings.

15. Educate Yourself:

Keep up with current developments in personal finance. Gaining knowledge of financial ideas might help you optimize your saving tactics and make wiser judgments.

Recall that consistent, deliberate planning, thoughtful spending, and smart saving are frequently required for successful saving. Customize these suggestions to your own situation and progressively develop a saving habit that supports your financial objectives.

Case Study: Jessica's Journey to Financial Stability through Strategic Saving

Meet Jessica, a young professional eager to achieve financial stability. Jessica's story serves as an illustrative case study, showcasing the transformative impact of strategic saving on her journey toward financial well-being.

Background:

Jessica, in her mid-20s, started her career with enthusiasm but soon realized the importance of managing her finances wisely. She decided to embark on a journey of strategic saving to secure her financial future.

Financial Challenges:

1. Lack of Clear Goals:

Initially, Jessica struggled with setting clear financial goals. She knew she wanted to save, but without specific objectives, her efforts lacked direction.

2. Inconsistent Saving Habits:

Jessica found herself inconsistently saving, often dipping into her savings for unplanned expenses. Without a structured approach, her savings lacked growth.

Strategic Saving Transformation:

1. Setting SMART Goals:

Jessica started by setting SMART goals. She identified short-term goals like building an emergency fund and long-term goals such as homeownership. This clarity provided a roadmap for her saving endeavors.

2. Creating a Detailed Budget:

With her goals in mind, Jessica crafted a detailed budget. She categorized her expenses, identified areas for potential savings, and allocated specific amounts to her short-term and long-term goals.

3.Automating Savings:

To enforce consistency, Jessica automated her savings. A portion of her paycheck was automatically transferred to separate accounts earmarked for emergencies, travel, and investments.

4. Emergency Fund Focus:

Recognizing the importance of financial safety nets, Jessica prioritized building an emergency fund. This fund served as a buffer against unexpected expenses, reducing the need to dip into other savings.

5. Exploring Investment Options:

As her financial confidence grew, Jessica explored investment options. She educated herself on basic investment principles and began allocating a portion of her savings to a diversified investment portfolio.

Positive Outcomes:

1. Financial Security:

With a robust emergency fund, Jessica experienced greater financial security. Unplanned expenses no longer created financial stress, allowing her to navigate unexpected challenges with ease.

2. Goal Achievement:

Jessica achieved her short-term goals, including a dream vacation, by consistently saving for them. NoHer long-term goals, such as homeownership, were well on track, thanks to strategic saving and investment.

3. Improved Financial Confidence:

As Jessica witnessed the positive outcomes of her strategic saving approach, her financial confidence soared. She felt in control of her finances and was better equipped to handle both short-term and long-term financial objectives.

Conclusion:

Jessica's journey highlights the transformative power of strategic saving. By setting clear goals, creating a structured budget, and automating savings, she not only achieved financial stability but also gained the confidence to navigate her financial future successfully. Jessica's case study serves as inspiration for others embarking on their own journeys toward financial well-being through thoughtful and strategic saving.

Chapter 5

Debt Demystified: Breaking Free and Building Wealth

Debt can weigh us down, but it's time to face it head-on. Assess your debts, prioritize high-interest ones, and strategize your repayment plan. Consider different methods like the avalanche or snowball approach. Negotiate with creditors and explore consolidation options. Breaking free from debt is liberating and paves the way to financial independence. Psychologically speaking, debt can lead to a great deal of tension and anxiety. One's mental health may suffer from the ongoing stress of controlling interest rates, avoiding late fines, and making monthly payments. Furthermore, the sensation of being caught in an unending debt cycle can cause desperation and pessimism.

However, debt might make it more difficult to achieve long-term financial objectives like buying a house or preparing for retirement. Debt interest can eat away at prospective savings, leaving people with little to no future financial security.

It is crucial to explore the complexities of debt and lifestyle creep in order to completely understand their effects. ***The following are some salient observations:***

1. Debt accumulation: A number of circumstances, including overspending, medical problems, or unforeseen life events, can cause debt to progressively mount over time. For example, using credit cards excessively and not paying off the balance each month might result in high-interest debt that keeps growing.

2. Lifestyle creep: The progressive growth in expenditure that occurs when income rises is referred to as lifestyle creep. People tend to update their lifestyles as their income increases by buying more expensive goods or treating themselves to opulent experiences. But if spending rises faster than income, it can quickly

become unsustainable and result in a very credit-dependent lifestyle.

3. Vicious loop: It can be challenging to escape the vicious circle that arises when debt and lifestyle creep coexist. People who have debt may feel compelled to maintain or improve their level of living, which encourages greater spending and debt accumulation. If deliberate efforts are not taken to address debt management and lifestyle choices, this cycle may never end.

4. Financial repercussions: Debt and lifestyle creep have an effect that goes beyond only short-term financial hardship. A poorer credit score from big debt can make it more difficult to get loans or advantageous interest rates later on. Excessive spending can also impede the growth of wealth and impede the achievement of significant financial goals.

To demonstrate the negative consequences of debt

The phrase "lifestyle creep" describes the steady rise in expenses that comes along with an increase in income. It's a phenomenon that many people experience and that can have detrimental effects, especially in terms of managing debt. A false sense of financial security brought on by lifestyle creep can lead to overspending and unintentional debt accumulation. We'll talk about lifestyle creep's risks and how it can eventually result in debt in this part.

1. False Sense of Financial Security: When people's income rises, they frequently feel more secure financially and may begin to indulge in things that they were previously unable to afford. This increased financial independence may cause one to squander on non-necessities, such going out to eat a lot, buying a bigger house or car, or taking lavish vacations. But this increased spending can easily become unmanageable, leading to debt accumulation.

2. Inflation of Lifestyle Expectations: Expectations on what constitutes a comfortable existence can sometimes get inflated due to lifestyle creep. For instance, someone who was once happy living in a small apartment might now feel the need for a bigger, more opulent house. The never-ending cycle of upgrading and

overspending that results from this never-ending need for more can pile up debt.

3. Ignoring Savings and Emergency Funds: When living expenses rise, people frequently put short-term financial objectives—like setting aside money for retirement or creating an emergency fund—below longer-term ones. Instead of saving that additional cash, it's being used for pointless experiences or goods. Unexpected costs or crises can rapidly put a person in debt if they don't have enough money.

4. Difficulty Adjusting During Income Reductions: When there is an abrupt drop in income as a result of a job loss, pay reductions, or other unanticipated events, lifestyle creep becomes especially challenging. It could be difficult for someone who has grown accustomed to a particular quality of life to modify their spending patterns. This may cause them to depend more on loans or credit cards to support their way of life, which will eventually put them in debt.

5. Psychological considerations: Social comparison and the need to stay up with others

are two further psychological elements that might contribute to lifestyle creep. One may feel under pressure to adopt or surpass a particular lifestyle after witnessing friends or coworkers enjoying it. This can result in excessive expenditure and debt accumulation in an effort to uphold a specific status or image.

Consider a couple, for instance, who just got a sizable increase at work. They make the decision to buy a new automobile, move into a bigger home in a posh neighborhood, and begin going out to eat at pricey restaurants on a regular basis.

Recognizing your financial circumstances

One of the first stages in controlling debt and avoiding lifestyle creep is evaluating your present financial condition. Examining your debts, income, spending, and general financial situation in detail is necessary for this. Knowing where you stand financially will help you make wise decisions and create a strategy for successfully paying off your debt.

1. Compile all of your financial data: To begin, assemble the required paperwork and

debt-related data. Credit card statements, loan contracts, mortgage information, and any other outstanding balances you could have are all included in this. Having a comprehensive picture of your debts will enable you to assess the scope of the issue and pinpoint areas that need to be addressed right away.

Consider the following scenario: you have three credit cards, each with a different interest rate and balance. You can prioritize paying off the card with the highest interest rate first by looking over each statement to see which one has the lowest interest rate. Over time, you can reduce your interest payments by using this strategy.

2. Determine your total debt: After you've gotten all the data you need, figure out how much debt you have overall. The total of all your outstanding bills, including credit card, loan, mortgage, and other outstanding debts, should be added. Having a clear understanding of your specific debt amount can help you to create a plan for repaying it.

If your entire debt is $50,000, for example, it is simpler to set realistic targets and milestones for paying it off. Dividing this enormous amount into more manageable portions can inspire you as you see results along the road.

3. Evaluate your income and expenses: Knowing your income and expenses can help you decide how much you can afford to pay down your debt each month. Examine all of your monthly income carefully, then make a comparison between it and your monthly outlays.

For instance, if your monthly expenses come to $3,500 and your income is $4,000, you will have $500 left over to pay off debt. You might find areas where you can make changes or cut back on spending to free up more cash for debt repayment by doing an analysis of your expenses.

4. Examine your debt-to-income ratio. This ratio is a crucial sign of your financial well-being. It calculates the portion of your monthly income that is used for debt repayment. Divide the total amount of debt payments you make each month

by your gross monthly income, then multiply the result by 100 to find this ratio.

Taking Charge of Your Money

Budget creation is a vital stage that we must not skip on our path to debt management and escaping the chains of lifestyle creep. Although many people associate the word "budget" with limitations or restrictions, in actuality, it is the key to taking back control of your financial circumstances. Knowing where your money is going and where it is coming from will help you make decisions that will help you reach your financial objectives.

In order to fully understand the effectiveness of a budget, *let's examine this subject from several angles:*

1. The attitude shift: Making a budget necessitates a mental adjustment. It's about making deliberate financial decisions rather than spending on impulse. Adopting a budget means that you are in control of your finances and are making them work for you instead of the other way around. You will be able to prioritize your financial objectives and make deliberate

decisions that are consistent with your values thanks to this mental adjustment.

2. Keeping track of your spending: Keeping track of your spending is one of the first steps in making a budget. This means keeping meticulous track of every dime you spend, on everything from a large purchase to a cup of coffee. By keeping track of your spending, you can spot trends in your spending, determine where you could be overspending, and make the required corrections. For instance, you might discover that the money you spend on takeout lunches every day adds up to a substantial monthly total. You can consciously decide to reduce your eating out and use the money you save toward a future goal or debt repayment by keeping track of this spending.

3. Establishing financial objectives: A budget is a road map for reaching your financial objectives. Your budget will direct you toward these goals, whether they be debt repayment, saving for a down payment on a home, or creating an emergency fund. You establish a well-defined course of action by designating

particular resources for every objective. If, for example, your objective is to pay off $10,000 in credit card debt in a year, you can divide that amount into manageable monthly payments and modify your spending plan appropriately.

4. Setting Needs vs. Wants Priorities: Using a budget makes it easier to distinguish between necessities and wants, which empowers you to make wise spending choices. When considering a purchase, determine whether it is a long-term ambition or if it fits within your financial objectives. For instance, even though you might be tempted to get the newest technology, it might be a better idea to put other expenses first if it won't improve your long-term financial situation.

5. Emergency fund: Establishing an emergency fund is an essential part of any financial plan. Because life is unpredictable, unforeseen costs can severely damage your ability to manage your finances. By reserving a portion of your monthly income, you build a buffer against unanticipated events. Consider the scenario when your car breaks down and you have to pay for the repairs.

If you have an emergency fund set up, you may pay for the bill without using credit cards or accruing more debt.

One effective strategy that helps you take charge of your money is budget creation. It gives you the ability to set priorities for your objectives, make deliberate decisions, and create a strong foundation for your financial future. You can escape debt and the traps of lifestyle creep by realizing the value of goal-setting, tracking spending, ordering necessities, and saving money for emergencies. Recall that creating a budget is about making deliberate decisions that support your long-term financial well-being and your values, not about putting restrictions on yourself.

Avalanche versus Snowball vs. Avalanche Method Avalanche vs. Snowball Method
There are several tactics that people can use to successfully manage their financial obligations when it comes to paying off debt. The avalanche method and the snowball method are two well-liked techniques that are frequently discussed. Both strategies have advantages and

can work well in various circumstances, depending on the financial objectives and personal preferences of the individual. We will examine these two approaches in-depth in this section, delivering a numbered list that explores the nuances of each approach as well as perspectives from other angles.

1. Snowball technique: Regardless of interest rates, the snowball technique concentrates on paying off debts by beginning with the smallest balance first. This strategy seeks to offer psychological motivation by enabling people to enjoy instant rewards while paying off lesser debts one at a time. People who successfully pay off lower quantities will have more momentum and confidence, which will keep them focused and dedicated to their debt reduction journey. Let's take an example where you have three debts: a $5,000 personal loan with an interest rate of 10%, a $10,000 student loan with an interest rate of 6%, and a $2,000 credit card balance with an 18% interest rate. Despite having the highest interest rate, you would prioritize paying off your credit card debt first

when using the snowball method. You would then pay off the personal debt and finally the college loan after it was settled.

2. Avalanche Method: Using an alternative strategy, the avalanche method ranks loans according to interest rates. By using this method, people prioritize paying off their higher interest loans first and only make the bare minimum payments on their other debts. People can save money over time by lowering their total interest expenses by taking early action on high-interest debts.

Following the example from earlier, applying the avalanche technique would entail giving the credit card debt, which has an interest rate of 18%, priority over the college loan, which has a 6% interest rate, and the personal loan, which has an interest rate of 10%. Compared to the snowball strategy, you would save more money on interest costs if you paid off the credit card bill first.

3. Things to think about while selecting a method: The factors that matter most when choosing between the avalanche and snowball strategies are your goals, personality, and financial status. If you have several smaller debts that can be paid off fairly quickly, or if you need fast wins to keep motivated, the snowball strategy might be more appropriate.

Reach Financial Independence

One of the best tactics for controlling debt and avoiding the trap of lifestyle creep is spending less money. Making compromises in our spending patterns can help us get financial freedom, even though it may seem difficult at first. We may take charge of our money and work toward becoming debt-free by figuring out where we can cut costs and being prepared to make the required adjustments.

Reducing costs can be viewed as both an opportunity and a challenge depending on your perspective. Giving up some luxuries or conveniences in order to save money may be seen by some as a sacrifice. Others could view it as a way to take control of their financial circumstances and put long-term objectives ahead of immediate enjoyment. From an objective standpoint, there is no denying the advantages of reducing spending; it frees up money that can be invested for the future, saved for emergencies, or used to settle debt.

Here are some important tactics to think about in order to successfully reduce spending and reach financial freedom:

1. Determine non-essential expenses: Examine your monthly spending carefully and note any areas where you might reduce it. This can be cutting back on eating out, cutting back on entertainment subscriptions, or finding more affordable substitutes for daily necessities.

For instance, think about meal preparing at home rather than dining out many times a week. This will encourage better eating habits in addition to saving money on dining bills. Likewise, pick one or two streaming providers that provide a large selection of content at a reduced price as opposed to paying for several.

2. Bargain with service providers: Don't be scared to haggle about bills and subscriptions

with cable or internet providers, for example. They frequently feature discounts or special offers that you might not be aware of. Furthermore, periodically check your subscriptions and cancel any that you no longer find valuable or useful.

For example, if you've been a long-time subscriber to your cable company, give them a call to see if there are any current specials or discounts. You might be shocked at how much money you can save just by asking.

3. Adopt a thrifty lifestyle: Changing your perspective about money can have a big influence on how much you can save. Look for ways to cut costs on regular expenses, such using coupons, buying used goods when you can, or going grocery shopping during sales. Imagine this: instead of furnishing your house with brand-new furniture, check out secondhand shops.

Investigating Further Revenue Sources for Additional Other Revenue Sources

A key to controlling debt and avoiding the trap of lifestyle creep is raising income. Finding new sources of income can significantly improve one's financial status, even though cutting costs and creating a sensible budget are crucial measures in managing debt. Diversifying one's sources of income allows one to build a more solid and secure financial future in addition to paying off debt more quickly.

Increasing income can be viewed in a number of ways, such as a way to follow interests and hobbies, achieve financial stability, and grow personally. To augment their main source of income, some people can choose to take on a side business or freelance employment. Some might decide to use real estate or stocks as a means of generating passive income. Finding chances that fit one's abilities, interests, and schedule is crucial, regardless of strategy.

In *order to further investigate potential supplementary income streams, the following tactics are worthwhile to take into account*:

1. Launch a side business: A lot of prosperous business owners got their start by monetizing their interests or abilities. A side company can

give you an additional source of income while letting you pursue your interests. Examples of these include creating a small-scale business, selling handmade goods online, or providing consulting services in your field.

2. Make the most of your skills: Do you have a gift for writing, graphic design, photography, or music composition? To make extra cash, think about doing freelance work in these fields. You may display your expertise and make extra money by connecting with people looking for particular capabilities through websites like Upwork and Fiverr.

3. Rent out assets: If you own property or have extra rooms in your home that aren't being used to their maximum potential, you might want to explore renting them out on websites like Airbnb or VRBO. By doing this, you can make money from underutilized resources and give tourists somewhere to stay.

4. Make sensible investments: Purchasing stocks, bonds, mutual funds, or real estate can all be profitable means of obtaining passive income. Investing can diversify your sources of income

and offer long-term financial progress, but it does involve thorough study and market knowledge.

5. Benefit from the gig economy: As the gig economy has grown, several options for people to make extra money have become available. There are flexible employment possibilities available on platforms like TaskRabbit, Instacart, and Uber that can be customized to match your abilities and schedule.

6. Make the most of your expertise: Take into consideration sharing your wisdom and abilities via coaching or teaching. Whether it's giving lessons to pupils .

Preserving Your Future: Avoiding Future Debt

Establishing an emergency fund is a critical first step in debt protection. Because life is unpredictable, unforeseen costs can come up at any time. In the event of an unexpected medical emergency, auto repairs, or job loss, having a financial safety net can ease your mind and keep you out of the debt cycle. In order to assist you comprehend the relevance of creating an emergency fund, we will examine its importance in this part and offer insights from several angles.

1. The value of having an emergency fund

- An emergency fund serves as a safety net against unforeseen costs. It enables you to manage financial emergencies without turning to loans or credit cards, which can result in excessive interest rates and debt buildup. Possessing an emergency fund eases financial strain and gives one a sense of security. It helps reduce worry to know that you have money set up for unforeseen events so you can concentrate on other areas of your life.

- In periods of unstable income, it acts as a safety net. Having an emergency fund on hand might help pay necessary expenses while you recover from a job loss or income drop.

2. Calculating Your Emergency Fund's Amount:

- Experts in finance advice building an emergency fund with three to six months' worth of living expenses. The optimal quantity, however, may differ based on personal factors like family obligations, health issues, and employment stability.

- Take into account your monthly outlays for groceries, utilities, insurance premiums, rent or a mortgage, as well as any other necessary expenses. To find your desired savings goal, multiply this amount by the number of months you wish to save for (such as three or six).

3. Methods for Increasing Your Emergency Savings:

- Start small but consistently: To start, allocate a predetermined amount each month that works within your spending plan. All contributions, no matter how small at first—$50, $100, or more—count and accumulate over time.

- Automate your savings: Establish a savings account that is specifically designated for your emergency fund, and have it draw automatically from your checking account. You won't be tempted to spend the money elsewhere in this way.

-Minimize wasteful expenditure: Examine your monthly spending patterns to find areas where you may cut back on or do away with unneeded spending. You can expedite the growth of your emergency fund by allocating these amounts there.

- Boost your income: To augment your main source of income, think about taking on a side job or doing freelance work.

Keeping up financial discipline is essential for controlling debt and avoiding the trap of lifestyle creep. It necessitates taking the initiative and committing to long-term debt management plans. Regaining control over your money and paving the path for a better financial future may be accomplished by maintaining discipline, regardless of the type of debt you're facing—student loans, credit card debt, or mortgage.

1. Establish a Budget: Setting up a budget is one of the first things to do while trying to keep your finances in check. This enables you to keep tabs on your earnings and outlays, spot areas for savings, and set aside money for debt payback. You are in a better position to manage your debt when you are well-informed about your financial circumstances.

Let's take an example where you have several credit card obligations with different interest rates. You might find that by developing a budget, you can put aside extra money to pay off the high-interest credit cards first and just make the required minimum payments on the others. Over time, this calculated strategy can save you money by lowering the total amount of interest paid.

2. Prioritize Debt Repayment: After creating a budget, it's critical to give paying off debt first priority. Prioritizing the repayment of high-interest bills will expedite your progress, even though you must make minimum payments on all obligations in order to avoid penalties. Imagine the following situation: You have two loans, one for a car and the other for school, both with comparable balances due but distinct interest rates. You will eventually save money on interest if you prioritize the loan with the higher interest rate and pay it off quickly while only making the minimum payments on the loan with the lower interest rate.

3. Steer clear of new debt: Staying financially disciplined also entails steering clear of new debt whenever you can. It's simple to become caught up in the cycle of overspending on lifestyle changes that are beyond your means or using credit cards or loans for pointless purchases. To prevent taking on further debt, instead concentrate on living within your means and setting aside money for bigger purchases.
For example, instead of using credit to pay for a new device you've had your eye on or a trip you've been wanting to take, think about saving money. By doing this, you'll not only keep your debt load from growing but also form sound financial practices that will aid in your long-term financial management.

4. Seek expert assistance: Don't be afraid to get professional assistance if you're having trouble keeping up with your financial obligations or if you're overburdened with debt. Financial counselors or credit counseling organizations can offer advice appropriate to your circumstances and assist you in creating a customized debt management plan.

Chapter 6

The Art of Investing: Strategies for Long-Term Financial Growth

A key component of personal finance that can result in wealth accumulation and financial independence is investing. It's the act of distributing assets—like cash, time, and labor—with the goal of making a profit or yielding a return. Before starting any investing journey, it is crucial to comprehend the many reasons why investing matters. Financially speaking, investing can assist people in reaching their long-term objectives, including retirement, college, or home ownership. Investing can generate a passive income stream and act as a hedge against inflation. Moreover, by giving needed capital to companies and industries, investing can support economic growth.

Here are some detailed insights to give readers a thorough knowledge of why investing matters:

1. Investing reduces inflation: Inflation is the overall rate of increase in prices for goods and services, which results in a decline in the purchasing power of currency. By producing a return greater than the rate of inflation, investing in assets like stocks, bonds, and real estate can help people beat inflation. For instance, if a person invests in a bond that yields 5% and inflation is at 2%, their real return will still be 3%.

2. Financial goal achievement is aided by investing: People can utilize investing to help them reach long-term financial objectives like retirement, college, or home ownership. People can build wealth and become financially independent by making investments in assets that yield a return over time. For example, by taking advantage of employer matching and tax-deferred growth, investing in a 401(k) plan can help people save for retirement.

3. Investing contributes to the creation of passive income, which is defined as earnings from investments that don't need ongoing management. Investing in equities that generate dividends, for example, might offer a passive income stream to augment one's primary source of income. Additionally, purchasing rental properties might result in a consistent flow of rental revenue.

4. Investing provides capital to businesses and industries that require it, which in turn serves to boost economic growth. Investing in a startup, for instance, can spur economic growth by helping the company expand and create jobs. Among the many benefits of *investing are fighting inflation, reaching financial objectives, generating passive income, and promoting economic expansion*. Before making an investment, it's critical to comprehend these factors to make sure it fits with one's risk tolerance and financial objectives.

Investing and Saving

Two of the most crucial ideas you should comprehend when it comes to managing your money are investing and saving. Despite their seeming similarity, they are very distinct from one another. While investing entails placing money into assets that have the potential to increase in value over time, saving is the act of setting money aside for future use. In order to optimize your financial resources and accumulate wealth in the long run, it is imperative that you comprehend the distinction between the two.

1. The Principal Distinction Between Investing and Savings

The primary distinction between investing and saving is what the money is used for. When you save money, you're reserving it for a particular purpose, like a vacation, a new automobile, or an emergency fund. Generally, your funds are held in a low-risk account that offers little interest and easy access, like a certificate of deposit or savings account.

However, investing focuses on using your money to attain long-term financial objectives. Investing is purchasing assets like stocks, bonds, mutual funds, and real estate that may appreciate in value over time. Compared to saving, investing entails greater risk, but it also has the potential to yield larger profits.

2. The advantages of saving.

There are many advantages to saving money. It first enables you to accumulate an emergency fund, which can act as a safety net in the event of unforeseen costs or a reduction in income. Secondly, it can assist you in reaching immediate financial objectives, like purchasing a new vehicle or going on a trip. Thirdly, by enabling you to pay for expenses with cash rather than borrowing money, it can assist you in avoiding debt.

3. Why Investing Is Beneficial

Investing offers several advantages as well. Firstly, it enables you to accumulate wealth over time, which can assist you in reaching long-term financial objectives like retirement. Secondly, it can assist you in overcoming inflation, which over time can reduce the value of your savings. Thirdly, it might give you a passive income stream in the form of rental or dividend payments.

4. Managing Investments and Savings

Although investing and saving are two distinct ideas, they are not incompatible. As a matter of fact, the most prosperous financial strategies combine the two. For instance, you may invest in a diversified portfolio of stocks and bonds to attain long-term goals and save money in a low-risk account to establish an emergency fund. In order *to attain financial success, you must comprehend two crucial ideas: investing and saving*. You can accumulate wealth over time and attain the financial independence you want by setting aside money for emergencies and short-term objectives and investing money for long-term ones.

The Secret to Profitable Investing

Having a good understanding of risk is essential to successful investment. When it comes to investing, there will always be some degree of uncertainty, no matter how much study or analysis you undertake. There is risk associated with every investment, and this risk can be impacted by a number of variables, including market volatility, economic conditions, and geopolitical developments. Nonetheless, risk-aware investors are able to make wise choices that support their financial objectives.

1. Categories of risk: Investors must be mindful of a number of risks, such as credit risk, market risk, inflation risk, and interest rate risk. Market risk is the possibility of losing money as a result of shifts in an investment's market value, whereas inflation risk is the possibility that your money's purchasing power will decline over time. Credit risk is the possibility of suffering a loss as a result of a borrower not making payments on their debt, whereas interest rate risk is the chance that changes in interest rates would impact the value of your investments.

2. Diversification: Among the best strategies for risk management is diversification. You can lessen the effect that any one investment will have on your entire portfolio by distributing your assets among a variety of asset classes, industries, and geographical areas. Your entire portfolio would be impacted, for instance, if you only invest in technology stocks and there is a slump in the tech industry. The effect on your portfolio might be less severe, though, if you had also made investments in other industries, such consumer products and healthcare.

3. Risk vs. Return: Investors must realize that larger gains are typically accompanied by higher risk. High-return investments, including equities and bonds from emerging markets, also frequently come with a greater risk profile. On the other hand, investments with fewer potential for return, such savings accounts or government bonds, typically entail less risk. Depending on your risk tolerance and financial objectives, it's critical to strike the correct balance between risk and return.

4. Time Horizon: Your time horizon should be taken into account when managing risk. Long investment horizons allow you to ride out market downturns longer, which may allow you to tolerate higher risk. On the other side, you might want to concentrate on assets with lower risk if you have a shorter time horizon, such as for a near-term financial goal like buying a house, in order to help protect your money.

Investing successfully requires an understanding of risk. You may make wise investing decisions that support you in reaching your financial objectives by comprehending the many forms of risk, diversifying your portfolio, balancing risk and reward, and taking your time horizon into account.

Choosing the Appropriate Blend

Asset allocation is one of the most important factors in investing.

The practice of distributing your financial portfolio among several asset classes, such as stocks, bonds, and cash, is known as asset allocation. Establishing a risk-reward balance that is in line with your investing objectives, risk tolerance, and investment horizon is the aim of asset allocation. It might be difficult to discover the ideal blend for your portfolio, but doing so is crucial to long-term financial success. We'll examine the art of asset allocation, things to think about when choosing your assets, and strategies for building a well-balanced portfolio in this part.

1. Think About Your Investment Objectives and Risk Tolerance: You must ascertain your investment objectives, risk tolerance, and investment horizon prior to selecting the appropriate asset allocation mix. The kind of assets you require in your portfolio will depend on your investment objectives. For instance, you might want to think about including bonds in your portfolio if your objective is to produce income. You might want to think about increasing the number of equities in your portfolio if long-term growth is your objective. Your willingness to accept risk in order to reach your investing objectives depends on your risk tolerance, which makes it equally significant.

2. Diversify Your Portfolio: The secret to profitable investing is diversity. You can lessen your exposure to any one asset class or investment by diversifying your portfolio. Investing in various asset types, such bonds, real estate, and equities, can help lower the total risk of your portfolio. You can further diversify within each asset class by making investments across several sectors or industries. For instance, you can invest in a variety of industries within the stock market, including consumer products, healthcare, and technology.

3. Rebalance Your Portfolio: It's critical to routinely rebalance your portfolio after deciding on your asset allocation mix. To keep your desired asset allocation mix, you must rebalance your portfolio by changing the percentages of each asset class. For instance, your portfolio may now consist of 70% stocks and 30% bonds if your target asset allocation is 60% equities and 40% bonds and the stock market has done well. You would have to sell some of your stocks and get more bonds in order to keep your desired asset allocation.

4. Think About Your Investment Horizon: This is the amount of time you intend to hold onto your investments. You might be able to take on more risk in your portfolio if you have a long investing horizon because you will have more time to weather market swings. However, in order to lower your overall risk, you might want to think about using a more conservative asset allocation mix if you have a short investment horizon.

Allocating assets is a crucial component of investing. You can accomplish your investing objectives and lower overall risk by determining the ideal combination for your portfolio. When choosing your asset allocation mix, keep in mind to diversify your portfolio, rebalance on a regular basis, and modify your asset allocation mix as needed. You should also take your investing objectives, risk tolerance, and investment horizon into account.

Mutual Funds Mutual Bonds Mutual Stocks

Mutual Funds Mutual Bonds Mutual Funds

The art of investing calls for a great deal of information, perseverance, and discipline. Choosing the appropriate investment vehicles is one of the most crucial parts of investing. Making a decision can be difficult when there are so many possibilities available. Nonetheless, knowing the various kinds of investment vehicles and how they operate can assist investors in making wise choices. We'll talk about some of the most well-liked investment vehicles in this area, such as stocks, bonds, mutual funds, and more. Along with examining the benefits and drawbacks of each investment vehicle, we will also offer some information that might assist investors in making wise choices.

1. Stocks: An investment kind that symbolizes a company's ownership are called stocks. Purchasing stocks entitles investors to become shareholders and the ability to cast a vote on corporate decisions. While stocks can be a terrific long-term investment, they can also be dangerous. Stock prices are subject to change in response to both the company's and the market's overall performance. When purchasing stock in a

firm, it's crucial to educate yourself about it and diversify your holdings to reduce risk.

2. Bonds: Bonds are an investment class in which buyers lend money to a government agency or business in return for interest payments. In general, bonds are less risky than stocks, but they can still be a solid source of consistent income. Bond values may also change in response to changes in interest rates and the issuer's creditworthiness. It's crucial to investigate the credit rating of the issuer and diversify your portfolio by holding bonds from several issuers.

3. Mutual funds are a class of investment that combine the capital of several individuals to buy a variety of stocks, bonds, and other securities. Investing in mutual funds can provide portfolio diversification without requiring extensive study on individual stocks. Nevertheless, mutual funds typically impose fees, which over time may reduce your profits.

4. Exchange-Traded Funds (ETFs): ETFs and mutual funds have a similar investment strategy of holding a diverse portfolio of securities.

Nevertheless, etfs can be purchased and sold at any time during the trading day because they are traded on an exchange much like stocks. ETFs have the potential to be more tax-efficient than mutual funds and a useful tool for portfolio diversification.

5. Real estate: Investing in real estate can be a terrific method to gradually increase your wealth and create passive income. Real estate investment trusts (REITs), which are businesses that own and manage income-producing real estate, are another option for investors in addition to purchasing rental properties. But real estate can also be risky, so before making an investment, it's crucial to learn about the property or REIT.

Choosing the appropriate investment vehicles is essential to gradually increasing your money. Investors can choose investment vehicles based on their risk tolerance and goals by knowing the advantages and disadvantages of each. Diversifying your portfolio and keeping an eye on your investments to make sure they still support your objectives are crucial.

Putting Your Money to Use

A key idea in investing that can have a big influence on your wealth over time is the power of compounding. The fundamental concept is that you reinvest the returns your assets make, creating even more returns in the road. Because the interest on your initial investment is also producing interest, this cycle of reinvestment might eventually result in exponential growth in your investments. This has the long-term potential to have a very strong snowball effect. Investing in mutual funds or stocks is an excellent method to benefit from compound interest. ***The following are important things to remember***:

1.Begin early: Your money has more time to compound the earlier you begin investing. Over an extended duration, even little investments made on a regular basis might accumulate considerably.

2. Have patience: The cumulative effect takes time to manifest. If you don't see significant short-term profits, don't give up. Follow your

investment strategy and give time to do its magic.

3. Reinvest your dividends: You can use the income from many companies and mutual funds to purchase additional shares. Over time, this can greatly increase your returns.

4. Steer clear of exorbitant fees: They will cut into your earnings and greatly diminish the compounding effect. Look for inexpensive market-tracking index funds, or ETFs.

5. Avoid attempting to time the market: It is a losing game to try to determine which stocks or mutual funds will do best in the near future. Rather, concentrate on and adhere to a long-term investing plan.

Let's take an example where you put $5,000 in a mutual fund with an 8% average annual return. Your investment would have gained $5,400 after a year. After two years, your investment would be worth $5,832 if you reinvested the $400 in interest. Your investment would be worth $14,693 after ten years. Additionally, your investment would be worth an incredible

$70,399 after 30 years. That is the mechanism by which compounding works!
Strategies for Various Life Stages:

Strategies to Fit Into Your Life
There is no one-size-fits-all strategy for investing. Adapting your investment plans to your current stage of life is crucial. Every stage of life has its own particular set of obstacles, objectives, and risk tolerance. While elder investors should prioritize wealth preservation, younger investors are more willing to take on risks. In light of this, the following are some investing techniques for various phases of life:
1. Early Career: You might not have much money to invest when you first start your career. However, it's crucial to get started early and to stick with it. Start with investing in exchange-traded funds (ETFs) or cheap index funds that follow the whole market. If offered, you may also benefit from your employer's 401(k) plan. Additionally, now is a great moment to invest in mutual funds or individual companies and take some measured risks.

2.Mid-career: Your pay rises as you advance in your work, giving you more money for investments. Reviewing and, if needed, rebalancing your investment portfolio now might be a good idea. Additionally, you want to think about spreading your investments throughout a variety of asset classes, including bonds, equities, and real estate. This can lower your exposure to risk and yield more consistent profits.

3. Pre-retirement: Your investing objectives should change from accumulating wealth to preserving it as you get closer to retirement. This implies that you ought to concentrate more on fixed-income investments that yield a consistent income stream, like bonds and certificates of deposit. Reducing your exposure to equities and other high-risk investments is something else you should think about doing.

4. Retirement: Creating a consistent income stream to support your living expenditures should be the main goal of your investing strategy after you retire. Investing in dividend-paying stocks, bonds, and annuities

will help you do this. Establishing a withdrawal plan to make sure you don't run out of money in retirement is something else you should think about.

Investing is a continuous process that needs thoughtful thought and preparation. You may attain your financial objectives and safeguard your financial future by customizing your investment strategy according to your stage of life.

How to Time a Market:

An Art

Timing is crucial when it comes to investing. Effective stock trading is a critical component of investment success. Here's where timing the market matters. Market timing is the art of forecasting future stock market moves and adjusting one's purchase and sell positions accordingly. While some investors firmly believe in market timing, others contend that it is impossible to foresee market moves with any degree of consistency. What then is the real story behind market timing? Here are some important things to think about:

1. It is challenging, if not impossible, to reliably time the market. Although an investor can occasionally make a profitable market timing choice, doing so consistently is challenging. The movements of the stock market can be influenced by a wide range of factors, including economic conditions, investor sentiment, and geopolitical events. It's difficult for even the most seasoned investors to predict every single one of these variables.

2. Timing the market is not as critical as experience in the long run. Long-term wealth creation ultimately results from time invested in the market, even though market timing may provide short-term advantages. Historically, despite sporadic ups and downs, the stock market has generally trended upward over time. Long-term investors can ride out any short-term volatility and reap the benefits of compound gains by remaining in the market.

3. One tactic that can lessen the dangers associated with market timing is dollar-cost averaging. Regardless of the state of the market, dollar-cost averaging entails putting a set

amount of money into the market on a monthly basis. This approach can mitigate any short-term market volatility and help investors avoid the traps of trying to time the market.

4. Investors can utilize a few market indications to help them decide when to purchase and sell. Although it is hard to forecast how the stock market will move in the future, investors can utilize a few indications to help them make well-informed purchase and sell decisions. For instance, the price-to-earnings ratio, or P/E ratio, can reveal whether a company is cheap or expensive. Technical analysis can also assist investors in seeing patterns in the price movements of stocks.

One of the most challenging and contentious aspects of trading is market timing. Some investors vouch for it, while others counter that it is difficult to forecast market moves with any degree of consistency. Long-term wealth building ultimately results from investment time. Nonetheless, a few techniques, such using market indications and dollar-cost averaging, can assist investors in making well-informed purchase and sell decisions.

Risk Management and Risk Optimization

While Optimizing Returns Risk Management and Return Optimization
Investing can be a challenging endeavor. To achieve financial success, an investor needs to sift through a deluge of information, decide which investments are risk-worthy, and assemble a portfolio that will support their objectives. Diversification is among the most crucial financial concepts. The process of distributing your investments over a variety of assets to minimize risk and optimize returns is known as diversification. For good reason, successful investors have been using this method for decades.

1. Risk management: Diversification plays a key role in risk management. You lessen your exposure to any one investment by spreading your money over a variety of assets. This implies that a bad performance from one investment will have less of an effect on your portfolio as a

whole. Let's take an example where you put all of your money in the stock of one company. You lose every penny you invested if the company files for bankruptcy. However, the impact of any one investment performing poorly will be lessened if you invest in a variety of stocks, bonds, and other assets.

2. Return maximization: Another reason diversification matters is that it might aid in return maximization. You have a better chance of making gains from various market sectors if you invest in a variety of assets. If you invest exclusively in technology companies, for instance, the performance of that industry will be your only source of return. On the other hand, if you spread your investments across a number of different assets, a number of variables, such as interest rates, the state of the economy, and global events, will affect your returns.

3. Diversification types: Asset allocation and securities selection are the two primary forms of diversification. Investing in a variety of asset types, including stocks, bonds, and real estate, is known as asset allocation. The process of

choosing which particular securities to buy within each asset class is known as security selection. Due to their ability to minimize risk and increase returns, both are crucial for diversification.

4. Investments in mutual funds that contain a variety of equities and bonds are one way to diversify your portfolio. Purchasing an exchange-traded fund (ETF) that mimics a wide index, like the S&P 500, is a another illustration. These two investments can help control risk and optimize returns by offering diversity across a variety of asset classes.

Effective investing relies heavily on diversification. You can lower risk and improve your chances of reaching your financial objectives by distributing your investments among several different assets. Diversification need to be a key component of any investing strategy, regardless of your level of experience.

Chapter 7

Income Optimization: Maximizing Your Earning Potential

Strategic planning and attempts to optimize your earning potential are necessary for income optimization. The following actions will help you increase your income:

1.Assess Your Current money: - Recognize the many sources of money you currently have, such as freelance employment, bonuses, salary, and other sources.

2. Identify Skill Sets and Strengths: - Acknowledge your areas of expertise, talents, and skill sets. Think about how you can use

them to your advantage for better-paying prospects.

3. Invest in Education and Skills: - To improve your skills, stay current on industry developments and make an investment in continuing education. Higher earning potential is frequently correlated with more knowledge.

4. Negotiate Salary and perks:- Discuss your pay and perks when you start a new job or in performance evaluations. Examine industry norms and make a compelling argument for your value.

5. Explore Additional revenue Streams: - To augment your main source of revenue, think about side projects, freelancing, or passive income sources.

6. Establish Professional Connections and Network - Making connections can open up beneficial opportunities. Participate in industry

gatherings, establish connections on professional networks, and cultivate ties within your sector.

7. Seek Career Advancement:- Look for ways to progress in your current role or investigate higher-paying roles in your field.

8. Firm Ventures and Entrepreneurship:- If you have a good idea, launch a firm or investigate entrepreneurship. This may open up limitless financial possibilities.

9. Improve Marketability: – Continually raise your marketability by keeping abreast of key technology, certifications, and industry trends.

10. Financial Investments:- To increase your wealth over time, think about making wise financial investments. Stocks, real estate, and other investment options may fall under this category.

11. Freelancing and Consulting:- Make your knowledge and abilities available for hire as a

freelancer or consultant. This can enable you to bill more for specialized services.

12. Create a Personal Brand:- Use social media and internet channels to create a powerful personal brand. Having a strong personal brand can help you land better jobs.

13. Diversify Your Sources of money:- Steer clear of depending just on one source of money. To build a more secure and resilient financial portfolio, diversify your earnings.

14. Continuous Improvement:- Adopt a philosophy of ongoing development. Review your objectives, competencies, and room for improvement on a regular basis.

15. Financial Planning: - Make thoughtful financial plans to maximize the impact of your income and maximize tax efficiency.

You can optimize your income and work toward reaching your financial objectives by putting these techniques into practice. Adjust these strategies to your own situation and sector, and take the initiative to look for expansion prospects.

Chapter 8

Building a Resilient Financial Plan: Weathering Life's Storms

Both individuals and organizations must navigate through different financial storms in the constantly shifting global economy. Financial resilience is the capacity to weather difficult times and come out stronger, from economic downturns to unforeseen calamities.

Knowing How to Be Financially Resilient

A complete strategy to managing and safeguarding your finances is necessary for financial resilience, which extends beyond owning a savings account. It includes the capacity to adjust to shifting conditions, bounce back from failures, and carry on pursuing long-term financial objectives. Now let's explore the key components that make up financial resilience.

1. Emergency Fund: The Cornerstone of Adaptability

An emergency fund serves as a safety net in case of unforeseen costs or interruptions in income. The goal should be to accumulate three to six months' worth of living expenditures in a readily accessible and liquid account. With the buffer that this fund offers, you can pay for necessities without endangering your ability to make ends meet.

2. Diversification: Reducing Investment Risks

Investing in a variety of asset classes can help you lessen the effects of market volatility. You can reduce your exposure to the risks involved with a particular asset or market area by diversifying your assets. By using this tactical strategy, you may increase the resilience of your portfolio and make sure it can withstand changes in the financial markets.

3. Financial Knowledge: Strengthening Judgment-Making

Making educated selections requires knowing the nuances of personal finance and being up to date on economic trends. People who are financially literate are better able to recognize possible hazards, negotiate challenging financial environments, and take advantage of opportunities. Continue to educate yourself so that you can make wise financial decisions that support your long-term goals.

4. Managing Debt: Reducing Financial Stress

One of the main components of financial resilience is efficient debt management. Pay off high-interest bills first and steer clear of taking on other obligations. You may better protect your overall financial well-being by putting yourself in a position to absorb financial shocks by keeping a good debt-to-income ratio.

5. Flexible Financial Planning with Adaptive Budgeting

While creating a budget is crucial, it's just as critical to be able to modify it in response to changing circumstances. You can reallocate resources according to changing financial objectives and priorities when you have an adaptive budget. Review and modify your budget on a regular basis to account for changes in your income, expenses, and unforeseen financial difficulties.

6. Insurance Protection: Defying the Unexpected

Because it offers protection against unanticipated catastrophes, insurance is essential to financial resiliency. Having sufficient coverage, whether it is for property, income protection, life, health, or other types of insurance, guarantees that you and your loved ones will have enough money during difficult times.

Building a Sturdy Financial Future in Conclusion

There is no one-size-fits-all definition of financial resilience. It necessitates proactive, all-encompassing financial management. Through the establishment of an emergency fund, investment diversification, financial literacy enhancement, prudent debt management, budget adaptation, and proper insurance coverage, people can strengthen their financial bases and confidently weather economic storms. Recall that readiness and flexibility are the keys to resilience, and they lay the groundwork for a safe and productive financial future.

A thorough financial plan must be created by following a few essential procedures. The *following guidelines will assist you in creating a customized financial plan*:

1. Set Clear Financial Goals: - Determine both short- and long-term financial objectives, such as retirement, debt repayment, emergency savings, and house purchase.

2. Evaluate Your Present Financial Condition:-
Compile data on your earnings, outlays,
possessions, and obligations. This picture gives
your financial strategy a starting point.

3.Create a Budget: - List your monthly income
and spending in a realistic budget. Sort spending
into two categories: variable (such as food and
entertainment) and fixed (such as rent and
utilities).

4.Emergency Fund:– Set up an emergency fund
large enough to pay for three to six months'
worth of living costs. A financial safety net for
unforeseen circumstances is offered by this fund.

5. Debt Management:- Assess your debts and
make a strategy to control and lower them. Give
high-interest bills a priority, and think about
refinancing or consolidation possibilities.

6.Insurance Coverage:- To guard against
unforeseen disasters, make sure you have the
right insurance coverage, such as life, health,
disability, and property insurance.

7. Investment Strategy:- Create an investment
plan that takes into account your time horizon,
financial objectives, and risk tolerance. Think

about spreading your assets across many asset groups.

8. Retirement Planning: - Put money into retirement accounts like 401(k)s, IRAs, or pension plans in order to prepare for retirement. Find out how much you'll need to invest for retirement in order to retain the lifestyle you want.

9. Tax Planning: - Learn about tax-saving options to reduce your taxable income. This might include using tax-favored accounts or deductions.

10. Legal and Estate Planning: Prepare an estate and take care of legal issues. This might include creating a will, designating a power of attorney, and taking asset distribution into account using trusts.

11.Review and Adjust Frequently: - Arrange for frequent evaluations of your financial strategy. As your objectives, earnings, or spending patterns evolve over time, adjustments can be required.

12. Ongoing Financial Education: - Remain up to date on issues related to personal money,

investment possibilities, and market trends. Having ongoing education gives you the ability to make wise financial choices.

13. Seek Professional Advice: - For individualized advice, speak with financial counselors or planners. They may provide knowledge and assist in customizing your financial strategy to fit your particular circumstances.

14. Adapt to Life Changes: - Have the flexibility to adjust to significant life transitions, such as marriage, parenting, or changing careers. Your financial plan should be modified to account for changing circumstances.

15. Monitor Progress and Honor Milestones: - Monitor your financial objectives on a regular basis. Celebrate your successes to keep yourself inspired as you pursue your financial goals.

Recall that a financial plan is an active document that changes as your circumstances alter. You may eventually attain financial success and stability by tailoring your strategy to your needs and objectives.

Chapter 9

Financial Literacy for a Sustainable Future

A competent resource for making acceptable decisions, financial literacy has been established; nevertheless, the impact of financial literacy on environmental sustainability has received less attention. According to the resource-based view (RBV), a company's performance and competitive advantage are based on both its tangible and intangible resources. In order to maintain their competitive edge, companies need a broad spectrum of resources and an extensive body of knowledge.

One of the key elements of financial literacy that has an international impact on the environment is *education.*
Various individuals have varied perspectives on financial education. If someone has a wide variety of financial knowledge, including the ability to comprehend complex macroeconomic concerns and how they affect daily financial

choices made by the family, they may consider themselves to be financially educated. Some, on the other hand, would limit their attention to simple, everyday money management. On the other hand, it seems that financial education addresses both broad and specific subjects. The expansion of sustainable development is achievable via appropriate educational channels. Society expects financial literacy in order to make wise decisions with respect to different resources. A financial literate population contributes to economic progress. Numerous elements, including social, political, economic, technological, and international commerce, have an impact on the environment. In order to establish a worldwide network across the many economic sectors, education and environmental awareness are crucial.

 For society to grow sustainably, each person must respond in a sustainable way. This is, of course, applicable to managing money and financial literacy. The significance of financial literacy for society is the topic of this essay. The Future Environment of Sustainability and

Financial Literacy Knowledge of finance: Financial literacy and literacy in general are entirely distinct concepts. Financial literacy and literacy are not the same things. Simply said, literacy is the ability to read and write. However, financial literacy is a comprehensive notion that comprises a variety of abilities, financial knowledge, attitudes, and behaviors necessary to make wise judgments for sustainable growth. In relation to social accountability and responsibility, financial literacy has emerged as a key area of study. Sustainable future environment: This refers to a state in which individuals may fulfill their fundamental needs without endangering the capacity of future generations to fulfill their own needs. Financial education is essential for gaining a better grasp of the requirements to battle climate change. Environmental sustainability encompasses a wide range of global challenges, including soil, water, and climate change.

The Value Of Financial Knowledge To Society Individuals' financial security is guaranteed by their level of financial knowledge. One economically significant metric that may be tracked globally is financial literacy. Financial performance, CSR, sustainable fiance, and financial education have emerged as key factors in gauging the expansion of the economy. In addition, the depletion of natural resources is one of the major concerns of our day. Financial education and corporate social responsibility have been linked in a number of studies. Financial performance and intellectual capital in the marketplace. Sustainability entails modifying the current business model to the dynamic economic, financial, social, political, and demographic environment while ensuring that finite resources—financial, physical, and human—are used sensibly and effectively in order to endure. Both the lives of people and the links between organizations and the environment need to be strengthened. Nonetheless, any kind of current undertaking as well as any kind of company (public or private). founded on capital, which is a basic item without which neither would be possible. Sustainability is not just a crucial component of public health; rather, it is a need for good health. The depletion of ecosystems, climate change, and the peaking of oil pose a danger to food shortages, resource disputes, displacement, and new disease vectors, all of which have detrimental effects on public health. At the same time, obesity and a number of physical and mental disorders linked to a sedentary lifestyle are at risk due to the overconsumption habits that are the primary source of unsustainable practices. This article examines the qualities and abilities that students must acquire in order to flourish and survive in the twenty-first century in a manner that promotes sustainability. "Sustainability literacy" is the abbreviated word used to describe these abilities and qualities.

The terms "environmental literacy" and "ecological literacy" come before "sustainability literacy." The emphasis has shifted from a limited concentration on environmental contamination to broader worries about how the ecosystem can satisfy fundamental needs for present and future generations. This has led to a trend where definitions of the new "literacy" have grown less focused and more broad in their meanings. As an example, let's look at Orr's definition of "ecological literacy," which serves as a starting point: A thorough grasp of how individuals and communities connect to one another and to environmental systems, as well as how they could do so sustainably, is implied by ecological literacy. Additionally, [it involves a comprehension of ideas like carrying capacity, overshoot, thermodynamics, tropic levels, and the magnitudes, rates, and trends of population expansion as well as the extinction of species. Understanding the workings of the contemporary world is necessary for ecological literacy. There is a close relationship between building and the environmental agenda. Therefore, there is strong justification for include sustainability in the building curriculum. Although there are strong governmental incentives to include sustainability into the curriculum, construction instructors' reaction has been inconsistent so far. On the other hand, the case study shows how simple it is to include environmental concerns into building training.

Cities' capacity to maintain themselves and the standard of living in them are being threatened by rapid urban expansion. Urbanization on a large scale has the potential to cause social unrest and compromise a city's ability to thrive both economically and ecologically. A new paradigm for sustainability is required, one that offers stronger incentives for reducing energy use, cutting down on consumption, and safeguarding the environment while also raising standards of well-being for the populace. Future cities need to have diversified social spaces with overlapping social and economic activity, with neighborhoods serving as the focal point of communities. To empower their residents to be productive and innovative in the socioeconomic sphere, they need to be developed or adjusted.In light of current educational practices, it is imperative that strategies for preparing the next generation to live sustainably be completely responsive in all spheres—politically, socially, environmentally, and historically. This necessitates a significant mental adjustment. Instead of producing more closed-minded specialists, we need to produce more open-minded generalists who can see the intricate relationships necessary to actualize such a way of life. Multidisciplinary students at Thammasat University have the chance to form and share their perspectives on sustainability challenges and long-term objectives via the Life and Sustainability course. The *overall results indicate that environmental protection, economic expansion*, and associated issues are becoming more and more significant in today's world. There is a shift in the mindset of the government, corporations, and students. Despite the knowledge, neither corporations nor institutions are contributing at a very high level. It was also shown that the majority of students understand the need for environmental education to be an integral component of the business paradigm. The current study argues in favor of emphasizing future thinking, imaginatively seeing the future, and expanding on the discourse around public empowerment and involvement in sustainability education. By examining and debating the views and learning results of the younger generation in light of their sustainable notions and models, the study closes this gap. Although the problems and difficulties that various cities experience are varied, ideas for addressing the sustainability concerns have previously been investigated. The term "sustainable city" is quite wide and has garnered the most scholarly interest in this area.

The importance of financial literacy for a sustainable future environment, as it relates to the rural residents of District Mandi in Himachal Pradesh, is a pressing issue given the abundance of opportunities people have access to in a variety of sectors, including the economy, education, entrepreneurship, and SHGs. The majority of working women and men in rural regions are well-versed in financial affairs and are aware of financial inclusion programs like the Pradhan Mantra Jan Dhan Yojana (PMJDY). Not only is financial knowledge not required, but understanding how to get, preserve, and protect our natural resources is also crucial for the development of future generations. One of the main challenges facing the economy is making the right financial use of resources to protect or improve the environment. In addition, raising awareness via seminars or financial education for everyone is necessary for the welfare of society as a whole as well as for everyone's financial well-being. Financial literacy seminars work to uphold norms of openness, justice, and customer service in the marketplace that respect regional customs and culture while pursuing a long-term goal of enduring win-win partnerships with all parties involved.

Chapter 10

Achieving Financial Freedom: Putting It All Together

Being financially free implies that you may go about your life without having to worry about being constrained by debt, needing an emergency fund, or thinking about money in general.

Here is a ***seven-point strategy*** that you may apply to help you collect money, become happy, and attain financial freedom in the next years if you're ready to become financially independent and free.

- **Start To Consider Money Positively**

Having an optimistic outlook on money is essential to getting wealthy and reaching financial independence.

Financial independence is attainable only by overcoming the mental barrier of negative money thinking.

The ideas that wealth is a sign of evil or that wealth cannot purchase pleasure must be banished.

You will attract possibilities and open up more doors than you ever imagined when you start thinking positively about money.

- **Rewrite Your Primary Financial Independence Goals**

Make yourself some money objectives.

Every day, go over and rewrite your objectives on paper, and consider how you may reach them. It will need five to ten minutes to complete.

Your odds of achieving your objectives will rise just by putting them in paper, revising them, and considering them before you go about your day.

- **Make Daily Plans in Ahead**

Make daily plans in advance. The night before is the ideal time to accomplish this.

Planning ahead for every day, every week, and every month will improve your focus and accuracy in everything that you do.

Working from a list can help you become more focused and will give you a stronger feeling of personal authority and self-control.

You will also be able to better regulate and monitor your spending habits if you plan each day in advance.

Establish where you will be able to save money and schedule how much you have to spend each week, month, or year.

From there, assign as much as possible to a savings account, an emergency fund, regular payments, and paying off any outstanding school loans. You may even think about creating a budget in order to participate in the stock market.

- **The Concentration Principle**

Every hour of every day, focus entirely on making the best use of your time.

To become financially free, you must adhere to the concept of focus.

When it comes to goal-setting and financial planning, almost everything you do is meant to help you identify the one or two things you should prioritize above everything else.

More than any other skill or habit you may pick up, your ability to cultivate the habit of focus will go a long way toward guaranteeing your success in personal finance.

Your primary areas of concentration and time should be directly related to your financial objectives.

- **Focus your attention on the things that will bring in the greatest money**.

Make an Investment in Yourself

In your vehicle, take in audio programming. An individual typically drives for 500–1,000 hours a year.

You have the ability to become one of the most learned and proficient individuals in your field by converting your automobile into a mobile university.

Invest in money management classes, study personal finance books, and browse internet financial publications. You may even invest in your own self-improvement by taking a financial advisor's advise.

Before long, you'll know so much about money that others will turn to you for guidance.

- **These Are The Magic Questions You Should Ask Yourself**

Following each significant encounter and life experience, pose the two "Magic Questions" to yourself.

The first thing to ask is, "What did I do correctly?"What would I do differently, next time?" is the second question."

You will improve beyond belief if you evaluate your performance right away after each meeting, sales call, and presentation.

Both of these questions have affirmative responses.

You may teach yourself to be even better the following time by thinking back on what went well and what you might do differently.

You may double or even treble the rate at which you learn, develop, and become better at what you do if you spend a few minutes after a call or presentation to write down everything that went well and everything you would do differently.

Your ability to perform better and become a better person will ultimately increase your income.

- **Show Others Generosity**

Treat every person you come into contact with as if they were a million-dollar client.

Every individual should be treated as the most important person in the world, both at work and at home.

Everyone thinks they are the most important person in the world, therefore when you treat them like that, they will appreciate your acknowledgement and respect more than you can ever realize.

Being a more giving person would undoubtedly make you happy and help you draw in more money.

It's a common adage that "money can't buy happiness."

Yet the fact remains that:

Having money is necessary for happiness.

Life satisfaction is predicted by material affluence.

Furthermore, we will feel more content with our lives the higher our economic standing rises.

Not only do our happiness metrics increase with wealth, but our overall feeling of well-being and life satisfaction also grow with income.

So, you will contribute to achieving more wealth and happiness by deciding to concentrate on financial objectives that inspire you and ingraining a good outlook on money, yourself, and life in general.

And once you do, research unequivocally demonstrates that giving generously with our finances makes us happy and wealthier!

How To Become Financially Independent And Save Money

Did you know that the formation of certain habits is the deciding element in achieving financial freedom?

Yes, it is.

Actually, the majority of self-made billionaires have already mastered these routines and have attained financial independence by perseverance and practice.

This is wonderful news!

Why?

Because you can become financially independent yourself by learning how to save money and think like self-made billionaires.

Some Money-Saving Advice

In this situation, which is very typical, I suggest starting small by saving only 1% of your salary and making due with the other 99%.

For instance, if your monthly income is $2000, decide right now to set aside $20, or.67 cents, each day.

That leaves you with $1,980 left over to live on.

Create a second bank account, your "financial freedom" account, to save money over time.

The money that enters this account may only go in one direction: within.

You never, ever withdraw funds from this savings/investment account or use them for any other purpose.

Its only objective is:

To facilitate your rapid attainment of financial independence.

Raise your monthly savings rate to 2% off the top after you are comfortable living on 99% of your income.

You will be able to live comfortably on 10% of your present salary in less than a year.

Continue doing this until you are setting aside 15% and eventually 20% of your take-home pay.

Because it will happen so gradually, you won't even realize that your level of life has changed.

But there will be a very remarkable shift in your financial life.

Individuals who are financially successful tend to acquire or cultivate a unique habit over time.

As *we become older, we are urged to save aside money from our allowances.*

But when we're young, we see money as a means to purchase toys, candies, and other items that bring us joy.

Because of this, we inadvertently start to see saving as a punishment, something that injures us and robs us of the toys, candies, and other things we want.

Most individuals start to equate saving money at a young age with suffering, giving up something, and losing out on happiness, contentment, and pleasure.

This bad behavior shows itself in our adulthood when we want to spend our money as soon as we have it.

Many individuals in their late teens and early twenties see each paycheck as a chance to go out and make as many purchases as possible.

For this reason, it's common knowledge in the restaurant industry that they'll be at their busiest on paydays, which fall in the middle and end of the month.

People start to equate saving with suffering and spending with delight at a very young age.

People tend to associate saving with sadness and spending with enjoyment because their underlying desire is to move away from pain and toward pleasure, discomfort and toward comfort, and discontent and satisfaction.

Utilizing Attraction Law to Achieve Financial Independence

When you start saving and feel good about your expanding account, the money takes on an energy of its own and starts drawing additional money into your life and into that account.

Long-time friends will reimburse you for debts you had long since forgotten.

You'll have chances to make more money than you would have otherwise thought possible.

You're going to sell items you've held for a while that you felt were worthless.

Furthermore, as you keep adding these sums to your account, it will attract bigger sums of money and grow more positive energy.

This is a remarkable finding.

For years, I had heard about this idea, but I was never able to take action since I was constantly broke.

Then, after starting my own business and, I ran out of money.

With my lifetime savings, I had been able to purchase a home, but now I needed to sell it to raise the necessary funds and move into a rental property.

That was the last day I ever went without money. I never ran out of money again, even though the economy was in the throes of a recession and companies were failing everywhere we looked. Every week, every month, I received business, the bills were settled, chances presented themselves, and it seemed as though wonderful opportunities were drawn into our lives.

I was able to purchase a gorgeous new home in a lovely neighborhood and move out of the rented house in a matter of years.

After two years, I managed to purchase a five-times-expensive home situated on a stunning golf course, with views of two lakes and the distant ocean.

Change Your Way Of Thinking To Become Financially Free

It's up to you to flip the wiring on this habit. It entails removing the wires from one set of attitudes and reattaching them to another.

It's your responsibility to start thinking about saving and accumulating money in terms of pleasure, and spending and getting rid of money in terms of misery.

The **Main Barriers To Financial Independence & Solutions**

Successful financial planning is thwarted by several significant mental barriers.

The most frequent explanation is that some individuals think they don't deserve to be wealthy for various reasons.

Now, I know some of you may be wondering, why is that?

Some individuals, like myself, have been reared with a continual drumbeat of harmful criticism.

This has caused them to assume, at an unconscious level, that they don't deserve to be successful and happy.

Of course, this is false.

Yet, this negative style of thinking may lead to detrimental financial behaviors.

These behaviors might be hard to break.

Change Your Attitude Toward Money

Negative events in childhood, which are all too prevalent, may have severe impacts.

For example, when individuals truly do triumph as a consequence of hard effort, they feel guilty.

These guilt emotions then motivate people to do actions to get rid of the money, to throw it away.

They waste it or invest it recklessly.

They lend it, lose it or give it away.

They indulge in self-sabotage.

It may manifest in the form of overeating, excessive drinking, drug use, marital adultery, and frequently drastic personality changes.

To alter your outcomes with money, you have to change your attitude about it.

You need to develop the mindset that money is a good thing.

Money is, in actuality, a lot like a lover. It has to be courted, enticed, pleased, and given careful consideration.

It is drawn to those that appreciate it, respect it, and can use it to accomplish great things.

It escapes from those who mistreat it or who do not grasp it as it passes between the fingers.

Believe That You Are Worthy of Money

It's common for folks to claim that they are not adept with money.

However, anybody can learn how to manage money well with practice.

Generally speaking, blaming someone for not being adept with money is only a justification or an excuse.

The individual in question just lacks financial success and discipline.

The individual does not know how to get or hold onto it.

Believing in oneself is the first step towards building wealth.

You possess an infinite ability to acquire all the money you would ever need.

Consider yourself a financial success in waiting for the right opportunity. And believe that whatever you achieve is yours.

Money Is Vital To Our Daily Lives

Money is a wonderful thing. You can live your life as you see fit because money allows you to make choices.

You may access opportunities that would not have been possible without money.

But obsessions may be harmful, just like anything else.

A person may lose sight of the reality that money is just a tool if they get too fixated on it.

Money turns become a negative thing if it is used to purchase pleasure.

In our culture, money is vital to our existence. In addition, it is impartial. It's not inherently good or evil.

The only factors that determine whether something is beneficial or harmful are how it is obtained and used.

Act Now!

To put all of these suggestions into practice right now, consider these two actions:

First of all, acknowledge and accept the fact that almost everyone with money today was once broke, and most likely for a very long period. They subsequently picked up the art of saving money, and now they are self-sufficient.

Chances are you can accomplish anything they have done.

Second, starting today, become an expert on money.

Examine it, learn about it, and apply the knowledge you get to your own financial situation until you start drawing more and more money your way.